THE CURSE OF KING TUT

Kris Hirschmann

ReferencePoint
Press

About the Author

Kris Hirschmann has written more than four hundred books for children. She owns and runs a business that provides a variety of writing and editorial services. She lives in Orlando, Florida, with her daughters, Nikki and Erika.

For more information, contact:
ReferencePoint Press, Inc.
PO Box 27779
San Diego, CA 92198
www.ReferencePointPress.com

Picture Credits:

Cover: tepic/iStockphoto.com
6: Associated Press
10: Relief depicting Horemheb (c.1323—1295 BC) before Horus, from his tomb, New Kingdom (panted limestone), Egyptian 18th Dynasty (c.1567—1320 BC)/Valley of the Kings, Thebes, Egypt/Bridgeman Images
14: Embalming in ancient Egypt (gouache on paper), Jackson, Peter (1922—2003)/Private Collection/Look and Learn/Peter Jackson Collection/Bridgeman Images
20: Anton Belo/Shutterstock.com
25: Egypt—1922: English archaeologist Howard Carter (1873—1939) and an Egyptian assistant examining the sarcophagus of King Tutankhamen., English Photographer (20th century)/Private Collection/©Leemage/Bridgeman Images
30: Maury Aaseng
34: Historica Graphica Collection Heritage Images/Newscom
39: Historica Graphica Collection Heritage Images/Newscom
43: Necklace with vulture pendant, from the tom of Tunankhamun (c.1370—52 BC) New Kingdomt (gold encrusted with lapis lazuli and cornelian), Egyptian 18th Dynasty (c.1567—1320 BC)/Egyptian National Museum, Cairo, Egypt/Bridgeman Images
50: zhaodingzhe Xinhua News Agency/Newscom
53: Associated Press

LIBRARY OF CONGRESS CATALOGING-IN-PUBLICATION DATA

Name: Hirschmann, Kris, 1967– author.
Title: The Curse of King Tut/by Kris Hirschmann.
Description: San Diego, CA: ReferencePoint Press, Inc., 2020. | Series: Historic Disasters and Mysteries series | Includes bibliographical references and index.
Identifiers: LCCN 2018056139 (print) | LCCN 2018057083 (ebook) | ISBN 9781682826324 (eBook) | ISBN 9781682826317 (hardback)
Subjects: LCSH: Tutankhamen, King of Egypt—Tomb—Juvenile literature. | Tombs—Egypt—Juvenile literature.
Classification: LCC DT87.5 (ebook) | LCC DT87.5 .H57 2020 (print) | DDC 932/.014092—dc23
LC record available at https://lccn.loc.gov/2018056139

CONTENTS

The Boy King

"When I started out for Egypt I had anticipated finding something, but I never dreamt that I should find such a tomb as this."[1] These words, spoken by George Herbert, the fifth Earl of Carnarvon, refer to the tomb of an Egyptian pharaoh named Tutankhamun. Discovered by an expedition funded by Carnarvon, the tomb was one of the greatest archaeological finds of modern times—and perhaps of all times. Filled to bursting with more than five thousand ancient artifacts, Tutankhamun's tomb was a treasure trove in much more than just the monetary sense. It also provided invaluable insights into ancient Egypt and a way of life that had been long forgotten.

A Short Rule

Even the tomb's occupant had been nearly wiped out of recorded history, but thanks to the items and records contained in the vault, archaeologists were able to bring this bit of the past back to life. The tomb was the final resting place of Tutankhamun, a minor pharaoh who had ruled Egypt from about 1334 to 1324 BCE. Although there is some ambiguity in the records, it appears that Tutankhamun—or King Tut, as he is more popularly known today—came to power around age nine. At first, Tut's kingdom would have been managed by advisers, but records show that as the boy king grew in age, size, and confidence, he increasingly took the reins of power.

Tut's physical prowess, unfortunately, never matched his powerful position. Although Tutankhamun was tall for his era, he was frail. He had a club foot, and he suffered from a crippling bone condition that forced him to walk with a cane most of the time. He was also repeatedly sick with malaria, a mosquito-borne parasitic disease. Already weak from his genetic flaws and frequent illnesses, Tut was in mortal danger when a broken leg caused an infection that spread throughout his body. Although scientists cannot say with certainty what killed Tut, the best guess is that a combination of malaria and this infection brought him down at the tender age of nineteen.

Erasing a King

Tutankhamun's sudden death caused a flurry of activity. Custom demanded that the pharaoh be given a proper burial. Accordingly, a small tomb was hurriedly created and filled with goods. While this was being done, Tut's body was mummified. This process, which took about seventy days, dried out and preserved the pharaoh's corpse. Upon its completion, Tut's mummy was placed in its tomb, presumably with all the pomp and circumstance considered appropriate for a deceased monarch.

As soon as the ceremony ended, the tomb's doors were slammed shut—and efforts began to erase Tutankhamun from Egypt's history. This was done because Tut, along with several preceding pharaohs, had instituted religious reforms that infuriated some people. Those who assumed power after Tut's death decided that these rulers had been heretics and they should be consigned to oblivion, a fate worse than death in the Egyptian belief system. Accordingly, the tunnel into Tut's tomb was filled with debris and covered with sand so the burial spot would fade away

Did You Know?
Tutankhamun's mummy still lies within Tut's tomb. It was removed in 2005 to undergo a CT scan, after which it was returned to its resting place.

This carved wooden mannequin of the pharaoh Tutankhamun was found in his tomb with a treasure trove of riches and historically important artifacts.

into the desert and be forgotten. Monuments dedicated to Tut and the other offenders were dismantled or repurposed to honor different pharaohs. Writings that mentioned Tut were destroyed; hieroglyphs bearing his name were chiseled off walls. Within about fifty years, Tutankhamun and his tomb had been struck from the records of time.

Emptying the Tomb

Forgotten by the world, Tutankhamun slumbered beneath Egypt's sands for more than thirty-three hundred years. Dozens of nearby tombs were found and plundered by robbers during this period. But thanks to the deliberate erasing of Tut's memory, the tomb of the boy king avoided this fate. It rested undisturbed until 1922, when it was finally discovered and opened by a team of archaeologists.

The treasures that spilled from Tutankhamun's tomb in the wake of this discovery were breathtaking and seemingly never ending. Each item had to be painstakingly catalogued before it was released—a lengthy process that resulted in a slow, steady trickle of wonders. These marvels were sent to the Egyptian Museum in Cairo for safekeeping, one by one, over the next ten years. The whole process was carried out in the company of Tut's mummified body, which remained within the tomb in its sarcophagus almost the entire time.

Watching and Waiting

The postdiscovery decade was a time of feverish excitement for the world's archaeological community. To some people, however, the whole situation seemed like an outrage. Tutankhamun's treasures were being snatched away beneath the man's very nose, with his body lying right there. An opinion grew that this was not merely disrespectful; it was robbery, plain and simple. If King Tut was watching from the afterlife—and some believed this to be so—he was, no doubt, enraged. He would find some way to take revenge on those who were disturbing his rest and stealing his wealth.

With this thought in mind, the public kept a close eye on anything and everything to do with King Tut. What misfortune would befall Carnarvon's expedition? How and when would the boy king strike? The world waited with bated breath for King Tut's curse to unfold.

CHAPTER ONE

Egypt and the Pharaohs

Long before the idea of a pharaoh's curse was born, the pharaohs themselves ruled ancient Egypt. Under their rule, the ancient Egyptian civilization lasted more than three thousand years and was one of the greatest cultures in human history. Understanding this civilization and its belief systems is essential to understanding the importance of the pharaohs—and the potential of a pharaoh's curse.

A Land of Kings and Queens

The pharaohs of Egypt were mighty, powerful rulers. Like kings and queens throughout the centuries and in many different lands, they usually attained this lofty position through birth. They were the oldest children or designated heirs of the current pharaoh. Nearly all were boys, although occasionally a female pharaoh rose to power. Once enthroned, a pharaoh ruled until death.

While the pharaoh lived, he or she had absolute power. This was more than just convention. Upon ascending the throne of Egypt, a pharaoh was thought to become semidivine. He or she was the living representative on Earth of Horus, the god of the sky and the protector of Egypt. This connection set the pharaoh apart from all other people. One pharaoh, Sesostris I, described his relationship with Horus with these words:

He begat me to do what should be done for him,

to accomplish what he commands to do,

He appointed me shepherd of this land,

knowing him who would herd it for him.[2]

Being the human representative of the gods was a heavy burden. Pharaohs were solely responsible for maintaining *ma'at*, or harmony, throughout the land. They did this by collecting taxes, making and enforcing laws, performing religious rituals, building mighty monuments, and engaging in warfare when necessary. They were also responsible for making sure the Nile River overflowed its banks on schedule each year to ensure a bountiful harvest—a tall order for a regular mortal but completely within the capabilities of a virtual god on Earth.

Ruled by the Gods

While the pharaoh wielded authority over the living, a whole pantheon of gods controlled the divine realm. Ancient Egyptian religion was polytheistic, meaning it recognized many gods—over two thousand of them, although a handful of these gods were much more prominent than the rest. Together, the gods were involved in every aspect of the world's functioning. They controlled the big things—the sun, the moon, the weather, the harvest, running water, animal behavior—and also small things of local concern. Each and every one of these gods had to be coddled to make sure he or she was watching out for Earth's human population. Appeasing the gods was therefore an important part of Egyptian life.

Daily rituals were one way to please the gods. In public temples, religious representatives might bathe and clothe statues of certain gods each day. They would also prepare

Did You Know?

In all, there were about 170 pharaohs of ancient Egypt. Menes was the first, and Cleopatra VII was the last.

meals for the statues. In private homes, small shrines served gods in a similar way. Families usually dedicated their shrines to gods of particular relevance to them. A family hoping to conceive children, for example, might maintain a shrine to a fertility goddess. A family praying for a good harvest might focus its efforts on an agricultural god.

At certain times, religious festivals brought all Egyptians together in communal worship. Statues of the major gods and goddesses were carried through the streets during these events. People gathered at the temples and left offerings of food, drink, and flowers. Afterward they could go home content in the knowledge that the gods were happy.

This tomb relief shows the falcon-headed god Horus wearing the conical crown of the pharaoh, indicating that the pharaoh was believed to be the representative of Horus on Earth.

Although all of these rituals were important, general good behavior was the best way to please the gods. As is true in modern times, ancient Egyptians had ideas about right and wrong ways to live. They believed that their actions were constantly observed by the gods and would eventually be judged. It was vital, therefore, that they try to live exemplary lives according to the standards of their society.

The Afterlife

The reward for these efforts would not come during one's current lifetime. It would arrive after death, when a person's soul had the opportunity to enter the afterlife. Guided by a jackal-headed god named Anubis, the soul would travel to a shadowy realm called Duat, where gods lurked around every corner and the moment of judgment was imminent.

The first stop in Duat was the Hall of Truth. Here, the deceased person's heart was placed on a scale and weighed against a feather from Ma'at, the goddess of truth, balance, justice, and harmony. If the heart was lighter than the feather, that meant it was pure, and the soul was allowed to pass. If the heart was heavier than the feather, that meant it was impure. The soul was devoured by hungry demons and entered eternal oblivion.

Those who survived the Hall of Truth proceeded to an interview with forty-two gods. Each god was charged with looking for a specific sin. The person had to persuade each god individually that he or she was innocent of the sin in question. If all of the gods were convinced, the person would be allowed to pass. He or she would enter the Field of Reeds, a pleasant realm where life was just like it had been on Earth, with one exception: death no longer existed. That transition, having been made once, would never have to be repeated.

Did You Know?
A work called *The Book of the Dead* contains complete instructions for navigating the Egyptian afterlife. It was considered a cheat sheet for the most important test of a person's existence.

Historians have commented that the Egyptian view of the afterlife—what other cultures might call Paradise—is unique in the annals of religion. It is not an idealized realm. Rather, it is just more of the same. As one author points out, "The ability to continue one's existence in essentially the same state as it was in the mortal realm spoke to a deep contentment within the Egyptians. They could not envision any place better than what they already had on Earth."[3]

Royal Treatment

Eternity spent in the Field of Reeds required the same items that had been necessities of daily living on Earth: clothing, toiletries, furniture, kitchen utensils, and other trappings of earthly human life. People therefore buried all sorts of paraphernalia with their dead loved ones. The richer the family, the bigger the stash.

Pharaohs had nearly unlimited wealth at their disposal, so it is no surprise that their burial caches were the biggest of all. Everything that the deceased king might possibly need or want was provided. Items buried alongside ancient Egyptian pharaohs included everything from dishes to jewelry, food to weapons, and board games to wigs. Some pharaohs were even accompanied by the vehicles they were thought to need in the afterlife. A pharaoh named Khufu, for instance, was buried with a 144-foot-long (44 m) wooden boat, for use in navigating otherworldly rivers. Tutankhamun had six chariots: three fancy ones for ceremonial use and three everyday ones for hunting, visiting, and other everyday trips.

The dead ruler was even provided with servants. In the earliest days of ancient Egypt, the pharaoh's actual servants were buried along with their king. In later centuries this was deemed impractical and wasteful, much to the undoubted relief of royal attendants. Clay figurines called *ushabti* were crafted to take the place of real people. Painted to resemble farmers, nobles, cooks, housekeepers, and all other workers, the *ushabti* would come to life in the underworld to serve their master.

Pharaohs were understandably worried about tomb robbery. They believed they would need their worldly goods, not to mention their mummified bodies, in the afterlife. The theft or destruction of these items would be a disaster. To deter robbers, therefore, many tombs were inscribed with dire warnings. One inscription, found in the tomb of a man named Petety, reads,

> Oh, all people who enter this tomb,
> Who will make evil against this tomb and destroy it:
> May the crocodile be against them on water,
> And snakes against them on land.
> May the hippopotamus be against them on water,
> The scorpion against them on land.

An inscription on a different tomb takes a more direct and less poetic tack. The owner states simply that if anyone disturbs his rest or his things, "I will wring his neck like a bird."

Warnings like these were not considered to be empty threats. The deceased, after all, were not gone for good; they still existed in the afterlife, and they would know immediately if someone violated their earthly remains. It was plausible that they could take action against such a person. Their curses therefore carried some weight—but not enough, it seems, to have stopped tomb robbers from plundering virtually all of ancient Egypt's tombs.

Quoted in Zahi Hawass, *The Golden King: The World of Tutankhamun.* Washington, DC: National Geographic, 2006, p. 148.

Mummification

Although all of these things were considered important, the most essential item in the afterworld was not jewelry, transportation, or servants. It was the deceased person's own corpse. Just as the pharaoh would need his belongings after death, he would also need his body, which was thought to be a vessel for housing the soul. As scientist Stephen Buckley explains, "The afterlife was just a continuation of enjoying life. But they needed the body to be preserved in order for the spirit to have a place to reside."[4]

A badly decomposed corpse would not do for this purpose. To be an effective vessel, the body had to be in the best possible shape and remain so for the longest possible time. Mummification was the answer to this problem. The first step in this process was to remove the corpse's squishy, quick-to-rot internal organs, including the intestines, brain, liver, stomach, and lungs. Only the heart was left in place, as this organ was thought to be the center of a person's being and intelligence and was therefore needed inside the body.

Next came a drying-out process. The now-hollow corpse and all the removed organs were packed in a salt called natron. The natron absorbed the body's moisture, just as a sponge sucks up water. When the seventy-day process was complete, the corpse and everything it had once contained were dry and leathery, which meant that the mortal remains would resist rotting.

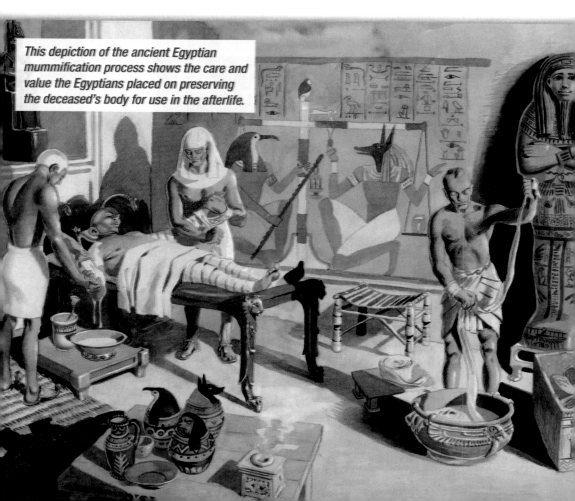

This depiction of the ancient Egyptian mummification process shows the care and value the Egyptians placed on preserving the deceased's body for use in the afterlife.

As the final step, the desiccated body was wrapped in linen bandages. Priests took great care over this step. They wrapped each toe and finger carefully before moving on to larger areas. They inserted amulets between the bandages, believing these religious artifacts would protect the pharaoh in the afterlife. When the first layer was complete, the entire mummy was coated in resin that dried into a hard, protective case. Then another layer of linen was added and coated, and then yet another. By the time the job was done, the dry corpse was encased in many thick protective layers that would, it was hoped, help the occupant withstand the ravages of time.

Hidden Tombs

While the mummification process was under way, the final touches were being put on the pharaoh's tomb. In the early days of the pharaohs, magnificent pyramids were built as final resting places. The famous pyramids of Giza, just outside the modern-day capital of Cairo, are the best-known examples of this type of architecture. The step pyramid of the pharaoh Djoser, which sits near the Egyptian city of Memphis, is another famous pharaonic tomb.

The pyramids were intended to be permanent reminders of their occupants' glory and power. They served their purpose well—*too* well, as it turned out. The pyramids proved to be a constant and tempting beacon, advertising the riches contained within. As Egyptologist David P. Silverman writes, "It was no secret that, as the burial process grew more elaborate, so did the value of the grave goods interred with both royal and non-royal mummies. Gilded coffins, amulets of precious stones, exotic imported artifacts all proved too tempting for thieves. . . . Robbers probably attacked royal tombs soon after the king's funeral."[5] Resourceful thieves always found a way into the pyramids, which were quickly sacked of their riches.

After centuries of coping with this problem, the rulers of ancient Egypt had had enough. Shortly before 1500 BCE, the pharaoh Amenhotep I instituted the practice of building hidden underground tombs in a secret location. Marked by nothing more than holes in the ground, these tombs were much more outwardly modest than the great pyramids of pharaohs past. Inside, though, the hidden tombs were just as jam-packed with riches as ever, and some were enormous. The largest tomb ever discovered had 130 subterranean rooms carved out of the desert bedrock.

Hidden Away

The new tombs may have been harder to find than the old ones, but that made little difference. Thieves knew that a recently deceased pharaoh had to be buried somewhere. A bribe to a well-placed official usually turned up the needed information. Some officials even worked directly with robbers, leading them into tombs immediately after they were sealed. The officials then split whatever riches the robbers obtained.

Did You Know?

Some historians believe that the Great Pyramid of Giza was constructed over a period of twenty years by at least twenty thousand workers.

Considering the ancient Egyptian belief system, tomb robbers might have had reason to feel nervous about their activities. They were, after all, stealing the property of the deceased pharaoh—a person who had now become a god in the afterworld. Since the gods were thought to be involved in every aspect of life on Earth, it made sense that a dead but furious pharaoh could wreak revenge on anyone who disturbed his rest.

Written records suggest, however, that this was not a major concern for thieves. In a confession dated 1110 BCE, a robber named Amenpanufer recalled, "We went to rob the tombs as is our usual habit."[6] He then went on to describe how he and his colleagues plundered a tomb and the bodies of the mummies within, then set fire to the corpses.

The most remarkable aspect of Amenpanufer's account may be its matter-of-fact tone. The robber had no apparent regrets or concerns about his actions. His confession, historian Joshua J.

The moment the doors slammed shut on a pharaoh's tomb, it was believed that the soul of the deceased embarked on an epic journey. The spirit descended into the underworld, where it met with a group of guards and gods. Together, this company boarded a boat that would carry them down a mighty river to eternal glory.

The path to this goal, however, was difficult. The pharaoh had to pass through twelve gates, each guarded by unpleasant and sometimes dangerous beings. To earn passage, the pharaoh had to perform tasks, such as answering tricky questions, feeding the spirits, or even engaging in hand-to-hand combat. The pharaoh's soul would also be judged on its overall worthiness and purity through a variety of tests.

The twelfth gate marked the end of the pharaoh's journey. After passing through this gate, the deceased ruler was reborn as Ra, the Egyptian sun god. In essence, he or she became the sun. It was easy for those still among the living to know whether the pharaoh had accomplished this quest. If the sun rose the morning after an entombment, the journey had been a success.

Mark notes, "shows how little these tomb robbers cared about repercussions from the afterlife. . . . All of the threats and all of the promises of punishment in the afterlife and terrible hauntings in this one could not deter anyone when, given the chance, they could break into a tomb and walk back out with a king's treasure."[7] Drawn by the promise of easy riches, tomb robbers were willing to take their chances when it came to incurring the dead pharaohs' wrath.

CHAPTER TWO

Exploring the Tombs of the Pharaohs

Thousands of years after the creation of Egypt's tombs, most had been opened, plundered, and abandoned. Modern archaeologists had an idea, however, that there might be undiscovered treasures yet to be found. Starting in the 1800s, they moved in to uncover the past—and perhaps even to find unimaginable riches still resting undisturbed. Like the tomb robbers of old, archaeologists were not deterred by the idea of a pharaoh's curse.

The Valley of the Kings

Most of the abandoned tombs were found in an area called the Valley of the Kings. This unassuming patch of desert, located near the modern-day city of Luxor, had been an important burial site from about 1539 to 1075 BCE. The Egyptians had begun digging underground vaults here, trying to avoid the rampant thievery that was such a problem for the pyramids and other visible tombs. Many pharaohs were buried in the Valley of the Kings and later joined by their queens, children, high priests, and important officials of the era.

The hidden tombs, unfortunately, proved to be not as hidden as the pharaohs hoped. Robbers continued to find and raid the pharaohs' burial caches. After centuries of this pillage, the rulers of Egypt gave up in disgust. They opened all of the tombs and removed any remaining contents, which they transported to even more secret group burial sites. The original tombs were left open and empty to the elements—and thus the situation remained for thousands of years. The denuded Valley of the Kings became something of an early tourism site, with world travelers popping in to see the abandoned tombs and scrawl graffiti on their walls.

In the early 1800s, interest in the Valley of the Kings revived. Egyptologists suspected that there might be more to the area than met the eye and that treasures might yet remain to be found. Accordingly, archaeological expeditions from around the world started to trickle into the region. They began to dig—and they were well rewarded for these efforts. Tomb after tomb was discovered over the following decades. None of the tombs were bursting with treasure, but they did yield an impressive assortment of smaller objects, murals, and a great deal of information about ancient Egypt.

By the turn of the twentieth century, the rate of discovery was slowing down. The Egyptian Antiquities Organization, which was in charge of excavations in the Valley of the Kings, gave a businessman named Theodore M. Davis an exclusive permit to work in the area. Davis's archaeological team made some interesting finds over the next decade, but the pickings seemed to become slimmer and slimmer as the years passed. By 1912, Davis was decidedly discouraged. He declared in one published article, "I fear that the Valley of the Tombs is now exhausted."[8]

Lord Carnarvon and Howard Carter

While Davis was excavating in the Valley of the Kings, other archaeological teams were working at nearby sites. One of these teams was sponsored by an English gentleman named George Edward Stanhope Molyneux Herbert, otherwise known as the fifth Earl of Carnarvon. Lord Carnarvon had begun dabbling in archaeology as a hobby around the year 1900. Increasingly interested in the field but recognizing his limitations as an archaeologist, Carnarvon hired a young scientist named Howard Carter to run his excavations starting with the 1907 season.

Working under Carnarvon's supervision and sponsorship, Carter made discovery after discovery over the next few years. He almost immediately found the tombs of two minor officials. As the years passed, he discovered many more important private tombs and, even better, the lost tombs of two Egyptian rulers—Queen Hatshepsut and Rameses IV. Carnarvon and Carter published the results of their expeditions to wide acclaim.

Buoyed by their success, the pair decided to explore a new area for the 1912 digging season. But their luck gave out, and this dig turned out to be a bust. One historical document explains that it had to be quickly abandoned "on account of the number of cobras and [horned vipers] that infested the whole area."[9] Efforts were moved to a new site for the 1913 season. Although Carter's team did not encounter any venomous snakes this time, the new site was also disappointing as it failed to yield any interesting results. Running out of places to dig and blocked from the Valley of the Kings by Davis's exclusive commission, Carnarvon and Carter seemed to be at a standstill.

This is the view today of the excavated entrance of Tutankhamun's tomb in the Valley of the Kings, which is near Luxor, Egypt.

This situation was immensely frustrating to the team. Carter was anxious to dig in the Valley of the Kings because he believed that the area was not, as Davis had asserted, "exhausted." On the contrary, as he explained in an article written years later, "we [Carnarvon and Carter] . . . were quite sure that there were areas, covered by dumps of previous excavators, which had not properly been examined. . . . We had definite hopes of finding the tomb of one particular king, and that king [was Tutankhamun]."[10]

Carter's belief stemmed from certain relics, discovered previously by Davis's team, that mentioned Tutankhamun. Davis thought the relics meant he had already found Tutankhamun's tomb, but Carter disagreed. He thought they pointed to an undiscovered burial site somewhere nearby, and he was eager to take a look for himself.

The Search for Tutankhamun

In 1914 Carnarvon and Carter finally got their chance. Davis had not made any significant progress in the Valley of the Kings for several years. Now certain that the area was empty of further treasures, he formally gave up his commission. Carnarvon and Carter snatched it up and prepared to search in earnest for Tutankhamun.

The search was delayed for several years by the outbreak of World War I. Carnarvon was stranded in England as travel through war-torn regions became increasingly difficult, and Carter's services were taken up with essential war work as a diplomatic courier. The Valley of the Kings rested undisturbed during this time. Although the war did not end until 1918, Carter had fulfilled his war-related obligations by 1917 and was ready to return to work. He headed to the valley with a team and started stripping the desert soil down to the bedrock, searching for the hidden tomb he was sure must be there.

This work went on for many years with no significant success. After five years, Carter's team had uncovered some ancient workmen's huts near the tomb of the pharaoh Rameses VI. They had also found thirteen calcite jars at the entrance to the tomb of Merneptah, another pharaoh. These meager results were disappointing to both Carter and Carnarvon, especially considering how much money was being spent. Carnarvon was footing a huge bill to employ Carter and all his workers, along with covering the expedition's expenses. As the years dragged on with little to show for his investment, Carnarvon became less and less enthusiastic about the search for Tutankhamun.

By 1922 Carnarvon's patience had reached the breaking point. He called Carter to his office in England to tell him that he would no longer fund any Egyptian excavations. But Carter, certain that he was on the brink of a major discovery, would not be dissuaded. He told Carnarvon that he would pay for the next season out of his own pocket if only Carnarvon—who still held the permit to dig in the Valley of the Kings—would allow him to continue. Moved by Carter's passion, Carnarvon agreed to fund one final season. As Pearce Creasman, an associate professor and the director of the Egyptian Expedition at the University of Arizona, puts it, "[Carter] got one guy to buy in and sometimes that's all it takes . . . to make something really big happen."[11]

Did You Know?

The tombs in the Valley of the Kings are numbered for easy reference. Tut's tomb is known in the industry as KV 62.

One Stone Step

Carter headed back to Egypt and assembled his team, ready to make one final push. The men began working on November 1. Carter's plan was to dig beneath some ancient workmen's huts that previous archaeologists had left undisturbed to avoid destroying this bit of the past. But Carter was out of options. He

King Tut's tomb was a treasure trove of riches. Arguably the most important object in the tomb was Tut himself. His mummified body lay in a sarcophagus beneath a solid gold funerary mask that bore the likeness of the boy king. The sarcophagus was enclosed in a small rectangular shrine. This shrine fit snugly into a slightly bigger one, which fit into a yet bigger one, which fit into a fourth and final shrine, like a child's nesting toy.

Along with Tut's remains, the tomb was packed floor to ceiling with about five thousand other objects that the king might be expected to need in the afterlife, including the following items:

- A full-size golden chariot
- Statues of people to act as guardians and servants
- Model boats for travel in the underworld
- Clothing, jewelry, and cosmetics
- Games, toys, and musical instruments
- Writing materials and equipment
- Weapons
- Beds, chairs, couches, and thrones
- Tools, lamps, and other household objects
- Food and eating utensils

Many of the objects in Tut's tomb included valuable materials, such as gold and gemstones. Others were made of common substances, such as clay and wool. But all of the objects, however rich or modest their makeup, were incredibly valuable from an archaeological perspective. Each one revealed information about a past that, until then, had been buried in the sands of time.

knew that the huts rested on one of the few unexplored sections of the Valley of the Kings.

By the evening of November 3, several huts had been cleared away, leaving a patch of bare ground. Carter went to bed that night anticipating a hard day of digging yet to come. As soon as he arrived at the dig site the next morning, it became clear that something was going on. The excitement of the moment is best captured in Carter's own words:

> The unusual silence, due to the stoppage of work, made me realize that something out of the ordinary had happened, and I was greeted by the announcement that a step cut in the rock had been discovered. . . . This seemed too good to be true, but a short amount of extra clearing revealed the fact that we were actually in the entrance of a steep cut. . . . I almost dared to hope that we had found our tomb at last.[12]

Carter and his men worked feverishly over the next two days to clear rubble and debris out of the ever-growing passage. Down, down, down the steps went into the depths of the earth. At sunset on the night of November 5, a twelfth step was cleared—and with it the upper part of a doorway that appeared to be blocked, plastered, and sealed. Carter was beside himself with excitement. "A sealed doorway—it was actually true, then!" he wrote later. "Our years of patient labour were to be rewarded after all."[13]

Digging Down

Although the urge to break through the door must have been overwhelming, Carter resisted the temptation. He ordered his men to refill the stairway with debris to protect his find. Then he dashed off a now-famous cable to his sponsor, Lord Carnarvon. "At last have made wonderful discovery in Valley: a magnificent tomb with seals intact: re-covered same for your arrival: congratulations."[14]

Upon receiving this news, Carnarvon immediately set off for Egypt. He arrived at the dig site on November 26. A total of twenty-six people, including Carnarvon and Carter, were present as the team got to work clearing the stairway once again. The

British archaeologist Howard Carter examines the newly unearthed sarcophagus of Tutankhamun in 1922.

crowd included archaeological professionals, historians, and architects as well as friends, family members, and laborers. All watched with excitement as the work proceeded quickly, and soon the entire doorway at the bottom of the passage could be seen.

It was instantly clear that the door bore the seal of Tutankhamun. This thrilling discovery suggested that Carter and his team had, indeed, located the elusive pharaoh. Their joy was dampened by the observation that the door had obviously been opened and resealed at some point thousands of years earlier. Nervous about what they might find, the team carefully unsealed the door and passed through. They found another blocked passage that had to be cleared. This job was completed by the time evening came, and the team found themselves facing yet another door, stamped all over with royal seals.

A great deal of politics were involved in the opening of King Tut's tomb. Egyptian law at the time stated that any treasure found intact had to be turned over to the government. The contents of a disturbed tomb, on the other hand, could be divided between the discoverers and the Egyptian government. It was therefore very much to the advantage of Lord Carnarvon and Howard Carter for Tutankhamun's tomb to fall into the *disturbed* category. Luckily for the team, it did appear that the tomb had been broken into soon after it was created, but it had been resealed with virtually all of its contents intact.

Or so Carnarvon and Carter said. Some observers, however, think that this tale is pure fabrication. They believe that Carnarvon and Carter entered Tut's tomb illegally before government representatives arrived to supervise the proceedings. These people claim that the archaeologists broke a few things and pushed things over to make it look like robbers had been there. They even knocked a hole in the wall between the main room and Tut's burial chamber to get an illicit look inside. Then they patched the hole and piled some reeds and baskets in front of the spot to disguise their actions.

Whatever the truth of the matter, the whole question turned out to be moot. Years of bickering between Carter and the Egyptian government eventually ended with Carnarvon's estate losing the rights to Tut's tomb. The entirety of Tutankhamun's treasure passed into Egypt's possession, where it has remained ever since.

"Wonderful Things"

The moment of truth had finally arrived. With a candle in his hand, Carter approached the door and made a small hole in the top left-hand corner. He inserted the candle, leaned close, and peered through the hole. His account of what he saw is one of the most famous passages in the written history of archaeological exploration:

> At first I could see nothing, the hot air escaping from the chamber causing the candle flame to flicker, but presently, as my eyes grew accustomed to the light, details of the room within emerged slowly from the mist, strange

animals, statues, and gold—everywhere the glint of gold. For the moment—an eternity it must have seemed to the others standing by—I was struck dumb with amazement, and when Lord Carnarvon, unable to stand the suspense any longer, inquired anxiously, "Can you see anything?" it was all I could do to get out the words, "Yes, wonderful things."[15]

It was clear, in this glorious moment, that Carter and Carnarvon had succeeded beyond their wildest dreams. Not only had they found the lost pharaoh, it seemed that unimaginable treasures awaited discovery in the long-sealed rooms lying before them. If any of the expedition members felt nervous about entering these rooms and disturbing the pharaoh's rest, they did not voice their objections—or if they did, their objections were not heeded or recorded. Apparently unconcerned about awakening an ancient curse, Carter and his team eagerly prepared to unseal King Tut's tomb.

Did You Know?
King Tut's tomb contained a dagger with a blade made from a meteor.

CHAPTER THREE

Strange Events

With untold glories lying before them, Howard Carter and Lord Carnarvon prepared to enter Tutankhamun's tomb on November 26, 1922. No one knows for sure whether the men were thinking about a pharaoh's curse in that moment. If they were, it did not worry them enough to stop them. They quickly broke through the sealed door and took a quick look at the contents of the first chamber. Then they returned to Carter's home for a celebratory dinner with their families, close friends, and colleagues, saving more detailed exploration for the following morning.

Carter kept a pet in his home—a yellow canary he had brought with him that season from England. That evening, as Carter's group enjoyed their meal, the canary met with a strange and unfortunate end. As reported later by the *New York Times*, "There was a commotion outside on the veranda. The party rushed out and found that a [cobra] . . . had grabbed the canary. They killed the serpent, but the canary died."[16]

Snakes were common in Egypt, and Carter probably thought little of the incident. Members of Carter's staff, however, were alarmed. Cobras were a symbol of the pharaohs. Was it not possible that the snake had been sent by Tutankhamun . . . or perhaps was even his living embodiment? They regarded the event, said the *Times*, "as a warning from the spirit of the departed King against further intrusion on the privacy of his tomb."[17]

Into the Tomb

If the canary's death was indeed a warning, it was not heeded. Carter, Carnarvon, and the team returned to Tutankhamun's tomb the next day. In high good humor, they prepared to enter the underground rooms. Archaeologist Arthur Weigall, who was standing nearby and observing the proceedings, is said to have been dismayed at the light tone of the moment. He felt that the men were demonstrating an unseemly lack of respect for the dead pharaoh and perhaps inviting danger as a result. "If [Carnarvon] goes down in that spirit, I give him six weeks to live,"[18] he reportedly muttered to a friend.

Undeterred, Carter and Carnarvon entered and thoroughly explored two chambers. The following day they found and entered a third room—the burial chamber of Tutankhamun himself—and then a fourth room beyond that. If the pharaoh's soul had indeed been resting comfortably for the past three-thousand-plus years, it was now well and truly disturbed.

Did You Know?
Tutankhamun's mummy was coated in layers of thick resin. Howard Carter was forced to cut the resin away, badly damaging the mummy in the process.

The level of chaos only increased over the coming months as Carter's team dove into the process of cataloging and removing the tomb's contents. Every day workers swarmed into the ground to continue a task that was so immense, it sometimes seemed impossible. In his memoirs, Carter recalls the overwhelming responsibility of clearing Tut's tomb: "This was no ordinary find. . . . The thing was outside all experience, bewildering, and for the moment it seemed as though there were more to be done than any human agency could accomplish."[19]

But the job must get done, no matter how enormous it might seem. So, day after day, Carter directed the piece-by-piece dismantling of Tutankhamun's burial cache. Each precious item was carefully preserved, packed, and sent off to the Egyptian Museum in

Cairo for permanent safekeeping. Although the objects were treated with care and respect, they were, nonetheless, removed from Tut's presence. This meant the supplies the pharaoh would need in the afterlife were being rapidly depleted. According to ancient Egyptian beliefs, if Tutankhamun were watching the proceedings, he was sure to be feeling dismayed—and perhaps even enraged and vengeful.

Carnarvon's Illness

People who held this view probably were not surprised in the slightest when Lord Carnarvon fell ill shortly after the tomb's opening. The illness started as a simple mosquito bite on his cheek.

The Tomb's Layout

King Tut's tomb is smaller than many of the tombs in Egypt's Valley of the Kings. It has four main rooms: the antechamber, annex, burial chamber, and treasury. A flight of steps leads to the entrance corridor and a doorway. At the end of the corridor is another doorway, which leads to the antechamber. The antechamber connects to a small room (the annex) and to the burial chamber. Connected to the burial chamber is the treasury. Although only the walls of Tut's burial chamber were decorated, the explorers found treasures in all four rooms.

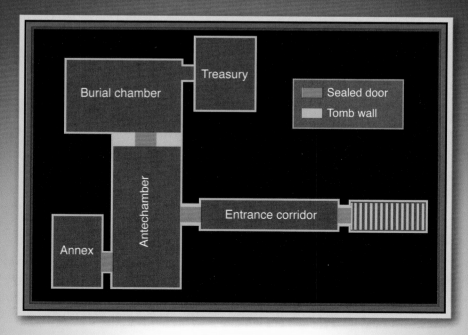

Treasury

Burial chamber

Sealed door

Tomb wall

Antechamber

Entrance corridor

Annex

One day Carnarvon nicked the bite with his razor while shaving. The wound quickly reddened as infection set in. Carnarvon tried to treat the area with the medicines available at the time, but they did little good. The infection worsened, and soon Carnarvon developed a fever.

Worried by this development, Carnarvon took to his bed for two days. He felt revived after this rest and was able to return to Tut's tomb. But he relapsed almost immediately and had to return to bed. Carnarvon's daughter, who was still present in Egypt, had her father transported to Cairo and summoned his personal physician from England. The doctor arrived about two weeks later, along with Carnarvon's wife and son.

By this time, matters had gotten much worse. Poisons from Carnarvon's minor wound had spread throughout his system. They had developed first into a blood infection, then into pneumonia, for which no good treatment existed at that time. Weak and delirious, Carnarvon proved to be beyond medical assistance. He died on the morning of April 5, 1923, a little over four months after first entering Tutankhamun's tomb.

Odd Coincidences

Carnarvon's death was the first major misfortune to befall the Tutankhamun expedition, so it naturally aroused a great deal of interest. People who had been nervous all along about a pharaoh's curse saw the incident as a sure sign of King Tut's displeasure. They started talking—and it turned out that there was a lot to talk about. Many strange things, it was said, had happened around the time of Carnarvon's death.

One of these things was the reported odd behavior of Carnarvon's favorite dog, Susie, back in England. Carnarvon's son, Lord Portchester, claimed that the dog had howled and then keeled over dead at the exact moment Carnarvon had died. He repeated this tale in many public speeches over the years following his father's death.

Another odd coincidence involved an electrical glitch. It was reported that as Carnarvon lay dying, all the lights in Cairo had flashed on and off several times. While this was happening, Carnarvon began babbling in a language no one could understand.

Yet another strange report involved the infected mosquito bite on Carnarvon's cheek. According to one report, the fatal bite was in exactly the same place on the cheek as a round scar on Tut's mummy—which was just the size and shape of a blemish that might be left by an infected insect bite.

All of these tantalizing bits of information combined to create a sort of perfect storm in the public imagination, explains Egyptologist Paul Collins of the Ashmolean Museum in Oxford, England:

> There's . . . the wealthy aristocrat who has everything going for him, who has found the greatest discovery in the world and then dies under mysterious circumstances. It's at a moment [in history] when people are going to séances to try to speak to the dead. And then you've got this mysterious world of Egypt, of extraordinary gods and goddesses and journeys to the underworld. Out of all that emerges the idea of the curse.[20]

Looking Back

With Lord Carnarvon's tragic example fresh in their minds, people started to look at past incidents with a new perspective. The canary incident, many agreed, had been a clear warning sign from an angry spirit. The howling dog, blinking lights, and precisely positioned mosquito bite were all highly suspicious as well.

But these things were just the beginning. Looking beyond Lord Carnarvon, people began to identify other past incidents that pointed to a pharaoh's curse. One such incident involved Jean-François Champollion, a French scholar who had first translated Egyptian

Hate Mail

The opening of King Tut's tomb upset many people. They felt that Howard Carter's work was rude and possibly dangerous, and they were not shy about writing letters to tell Carter how they felt.

One letter came from a woman named Marie Coleman, who claimed to be a "divine prophetess and messenger of God." Regarding Carnarvon's death, she wrote, "King Tut told me he was going to control this insect and make it sting the Earl. . . . If I had been able to get a message to your Mate I could have saved his life."

Another woman named Margit Labouchere wrote several letters. "Nobody is allowed to open the coffin. Listen to your inward voice," she warned in one of her missives. In another, she passed on a more cryptic message. "It is not the vengeance of Tot.ench.amon. I, only I, know the secret," she wrote.

Carter saved many of these letters, which were auctioned off in 2012. The historic stash, said auctioneer Simon Roberts, "has been kept by the family ever since [Carter] died and is very important because it completes the picture." Roberts likened these letters to modern-day social media frenzies. "Today [people] would probably contact him through Twitter," he said in a 2012 interview. It is fortunate for the historical record that these communications were produced in a more lasting medium.

Quoted in Chris Hanlon, "'Nobody Is Allowed to Open the Coffin,'" *Daily Mail* (London), May 18, 2012. www.dailymail.co.uk.

hieroglyphics during the early 1800s. Champollion had dropped dead of a stroke at age forty-one while preparing a summary of his investigations in Egypt. This untimely death, some said, was the result of an ancient Egyptian curse. The pharaohs clearly did not want their secrets translated and revealed to the world.

Another incident had occurred during the late 1800s, when an archaeological team went to open a tomb at a site called Meidum. The tomb contained certain statues that had allegedly been forbidden by the pharaoh who ruled at the time of their construction. According to some sources, the first workman to enter the tomb had gazed deep into the lifelike inlaid crystal eyes of these magnificent figures—then screamed and dropped dead of a heart attack. Merely looking at the forbidden objects had apparently aroused the wrath of the dead pharaoh.

Mystery and Tragedy

The curious eyes of the world were now fixed firmly on the Tutankhamun expedition, and it did not take long for more evidence of a curse to appear. A few weeks after Carnarvon's death, Carter gave a personal tour of Tut's tomb to a wealthy businessman named George J. Gould. Gould almost immediately came down with a mysterious fever. He died on May 16, 1923, about six weeks after Carnarvon's passing.

The next untimely death occurred the following month. Philip Livingstone Poe, a relative of the writer Edgar Allan Poe, had also visited King Tut's tomb. Shortly afterward he contracted pneumonia and died. "Ever since the Poes returned from their tour their friends have been jokingly warning them of the 'mummy's curse.' The joking wore off, however, when Mr. Poe became ill,"[21] wrote the New York Times, which had quickly picked up on the story.

Yet another visitor to meet a sudden end was Joel Woolf, a British financier. Woolf had been one of the first members of the public to enter Tut's tomb. Only thirty years old, he was fit, healthy, and apparently in the prime of life. Nonetheless, one night, Woolf slipped

Workers remove some of the items found in Tutankhamun's tomb. As a number of workers and others began to fall deathly ill or experience strange accidents over the ensuing months, the rumor of Tutankhamun's curse became widespread.

Archaeologist . . . or Thief?

Howard Carter was an extraordinarily competent archaeologist for his time, documenting everything in Tut's tomb with impressive precision. Some people believe, however, that Carter left a few things out of his meticulous notes. They are convinced that Carter kept some of Tutankhamun's treasures for himself. To put it more bluntly, they say he stole things from the tomb.

To support this claim, people point to previously unknown Tutankhamun artifacts that have turned up in museum collections around the world. "All objects from the tomb should be in Egypt, and if they're not in Egypt, they didn't get out legally," explains Christian Loeben, an Egyptologist at the August Kestner Museum in the German city of Hanover. Loeben contends that Carter was responsible for this illicit export.

Loeben does not think Carter stole items with the idea of selling them. "The artifacts would only have become really valuable if he had admitted they came from Tutankhamun's tomb, and he couldn't say that. I would say he took a few things for himself and members of his team and Lord Carnarvon as souvenirs," he says.

Whatever Carter's motivations may have been, any unauthorized removal of Tut's treasures would have been theft—and this act would have made Carter a tomb robber, no better than the tomb robbers of yore.

Quoted in David Crossland, "Howard Carter 'Stole from Tomb of Tutankhamun,'" *National* (Abu Dhabi), January 21, 2010. www.thenational.ae.

into a coma for no apparent reason and died soon afterward. It was all too easy to blame a vengeful spirit for his mysterious death.

A fourth victim was an Egyptian prince named Ali Kamel Fahmy Bey who, like Gould, had visited Tut's tomb as the guest of Carter. Soon after this visit, Bey and his wife, Marguerite, got into a heated argument. The tiff quickly spun out of control, and at 2:30 a.m. on July 10, Marguerite shot her husband several times in the neck, back, and head. Bey's subsequent death was highly publicized, and his presence in King Tut's tomb shortly before his demise did not go unnoticed. Tutankhamun's malign influence, some people said, had driven Marguerite insane, causing the unfortunate incident.

A fifth story emerged within a year of the opening of Tutankhamun's tomb. Lord Carnarvon's half brother, Aubrey Herbert, had visited the archaeological site to watch his brother's team at work. Just before entering Tut's burial chamber, Herbert is reported to have turned to a companion and laughingly said, "Something dreadful is going to happen to our family."[22] He turned out to be right. Herbert had always had very poor eyesight, but soon after returning home from Egypt he became almost totally blind. He underwent surgery to correct the problem but ended up with a severe infection as a result. He died on September 23, 1923, just over five months after his older half brother had drawn his last breath.

Staying the Course

All of these incidents might have worried some people. As the man who had found Tutankhamun's tomb and disturbed its peace, Howard Carter might have been expected to feel some concern for his personal safety. But this does not seem to have been the case. During the course of the year following the tomb's opening, Carter continued to enter Tut's chambers each day and work on cataloging the contents. His health did not suffer, and he did not meet with any shocking accidents.

In a memoir published some years later, Carter described his feelings about the so-called curse. "It has been stated in various quarters that there are actual physical dangers hidden in [Tutankhamun's] tomb—mysterious forces, called into being by some malefic power, to take vengeance against whomsoever should dare to pass its portals. There was perhaps no place in the world freer from risks than the tomb," he stated emphatically. "All sane persons should dismiss such inventions with contempt."[23]

Immediately after the discovery of Tut's tomb, Carter's viewpoint might have held some weight with observers. As the first year wore on and the death toll continued to rise, however, people became more and more convinced that something supernatural was going on. Writer Mark Beynon describes the general uneasiness surrounding Tutankhamun: "It is certainly difficult to ignore the fact that something peculiar was going on in Luxor, and the tomb of King Tut seemed to be at the epicentre of all the singular happenings."[24] The world watched, fascinated and fearful, wondering what misfortune would next befall Howard Carter and his ill-fated expedition.

CHAPTER FOUR

The Story Grows

Everyone loves a good ghost story, and during the late 1920s, tales of a pharaoh's curse certainly fit the bill. The thought of a dead Egyptian spirit taking revenge on the living was exciting and creepy. As odd happenings and coincidences started to swirl around the Tutankhamun expedition, it even started to seem plausible. With each new incident and bit of information flowing out of Egypt, the idea of a pharaoh's curse—and, in particular, the idea of King Tut's curse—grew to bigger and bigger proportions.

An Exclusive Deal

The frenzy of public interest had arisen immediately after Tutankhamun's tomb had been opened. Members of the public and the press had descended upon Carter's work site in droves. They had hoped to see a fabulous artifact being lifted from the tomb or to hear an excited shout from a worker unearthing a new discovery. Although flattering, all of this attention had been very distracting to Carter and his team. "Archaeology under the spotlight is a new and rather bewildering experience for most of us," Carter confessed in an interview at the time. He went on to describe how reporters were stalking him and his workmen, even to the point of hiding "around corners to surprise a secret out of us."[25]

To resolve this situation, Lord Carnarvon had struck an unprecedented deal with the London newspaper the *Times* before his illness and death. In return for a substantial fee, he had granted the newspaper the exclusive rights to all coverage of the activities at Tut's tomb. This meant that only *Times* personnel would receive tomb access, official interviews, and photography permission. All other news outlets would be shut out of the information chain.

With this deal, Carnarvon had hoped to shut down the circus-like atmosphere around Tutankhamun's tomb and give Carter's team some much-needed breathing room. The effect, unfortunately, was not quite what Carnarvon had anticipated. Instead of walking away quietly, reporters and news outlets from all around the world were dizzy with rage. They could not bear to be cut out of the biggest archaeological find of the century—perhaps even the millennium. Furious with Carnarvon and Carter, and desperate to participate in the growing Tut frenzy, publications everywhere went on the hunt for scraps of information.

Dire Warnings

One of the first such scraps was printed while Lord Carnarvon rested in his sickbed in Cairo. On March 24, 1923, a newsletter called the *Daily Express* published a report on Lord Carnarvon's failing health. The report included remarks from a popular novelist of the time named Marie Corelli. Corelli was fascinated by anything having to do with the occult, magic, and mysticism. "I cannot but think that some risks are run by breaking into the last rest of a king of Egypt whose tomb is specially and solemnly guarded, and robbing him of possessions," she commented. "This is why I ask: was it a mosquito bite that has so seriously infected Lord Carnarvon?"[26]

When Carnarvon died two weeks later, people remembered Corelli's words. The writer was hailed as clairvoyant, knowledgeable in the ways of the afterworld. Not one to let an opportunity pass, Corelli offered more observations. She claimed that a threatening phrase—"Death comes on wings to he who enters the tomb of a pharaoh"—was carved over the entrance to Tutankhamun's tomb. Although no evidence of such an inscription was ever found, Corelli's readers believed it. The tale was repeated so often that it became accepted as a fact—and a most disturbing one, at that.

British tourists arrive at Tutankhamun's tomb on donkeys. News of the tomb's discovery and its fabulous contents caused a flurry of curious tourists to descend on the dig.

Sir Arthur Conan Doyle, another famous writer with an interest in the occult, added to the growing buzz surrounding Carnarvon's death. Earlier in 1923 Conan Doyle had given an interview claiming that his friend Bertram Fletcher Robinson had been the victim of a mummy's curse. Robinson, who was a newspaper editor, had been studying a mummy in the British Museum for research prior to writing some articles. Conan Doyle said that he had warned his friend to desist and told him he was tempting fate with his activities. But Robinson continued—and then fell ill and died. "The immediate cause of his death was typhoid fever, but that is the way in which the 'elementals' [nature spirits] guarding the mummy might act,"[27] Conan Doyle speculated.

When Carnarvon passed away, reporters recalled what Conan Doyle had said. They approached the author and asked whether he thought the same "elementals" that had caused Robinson's

The earliest stories about a pharaoh's curse were just that—stories. Perhaps the first fictional foray into this realm was Jane Webb Loudon's enthusiastically titled *The Mummy! A Tale of the Twenty-Second Century* (1827), a three-volume novel that concerned an Egyptian mummy named Cheops. Brought back to life in the year 2126, Cheops is not evil; he is essentially a good guy. However, the idea of a mummy's reanimation was a first, and it laid fertile groundwork for the gorier imaginings of later authors.

Another classic entry into the mummy genre was published in 1869. Written by now-famous author Louisa May Alcott of *Little Men* and *Little Women* fame, the short story "Lost in a Pyramid; or The Mummy's Curse" concerns an explorer who uses a mummified body part as a torch while trying to find his way into an Egyptian pyramid. The priestess who once owned this body part now inhabits the afterworld, and she is understandably annoyed by the explorer's rudeness. She curses some seeds the explorer finds in the heart of the pyramid. The explorer takes the seeds back to America and gives them to his fiancée, who plants them. They bloom into flowers that the woman wears at her wedding—but cursed fumes from the blossoms send her into a coma from which she never awakes.

death might have also killed Carnarvon. Conan Doyle briefly agreed that this might, indeed, have been the case. The *Daily Express* reported Conan Doyle's comments, which were accepted by an increasingly interested—and unquestioning—public.

Fabricated Stories

Newspaper publishers soon realized the true value of the pharaoh's curse. Readers would pay for newspapers that reported stories—any stories—connected with Tutankhamun's tomb. The more spectacular and implausible the story, the better. Only the *Times* had authoritative information, but others were happy to speculate and sensationalize if it captured a share of the reading public. Encouraged by the positive reaction to the interviews with Corelli and Conan Doyle, news outlets solicited comments from others about the so-called curse of King Tut. They printed the words of anyone who supported the idea in any way.

One example appeared in the *St. Louis Post-Dispatch* in March 1923. The article's author had interviewed Sir Ernest Budge, the keeper of the Egyptian section at the British Museum. Budge had reportedly laughed in derision when asked whether King Tut's curse was real. He qualified this dismissal, however. "I wouldn't myself disturb a mummy in its tomb," he admitted. "I wouldn't mind taking some article from the tomb, but as for the mummy itself—I'd leave it alone."[28]

It is impossible to tell from the article exactly what Budge meant because the text did not elaborate or explain the comment in any way. Perhaps Budge meant that he considered it disrespectful to handle any person's mortal remains. Maybe he was worried about damaging the mummy and was speaking from a perspective of archaeological concern. Whatever Budge's true intent, the article presented his words as an endorsement of the idea of King Tut's curse. "Ancient Curse Recalled by Lord Carnarvon's Illness. . . . Superstitious Fear 'Voodoo' for Those Who Disturb Pharaohs' Sleep,"[29] the headline screamed. People bought the paper, read the article, and came away more convinced than ever that King Tut's curse was real.

At least the *Post-Dispatch*, in this instance, had actually interviewed someone who was in a position to speak on the subject of Egyptian tombs. Other news sources were not as discriminating in their practices. If they could not find anyone to interview, they just made things up. One English lord who passed away, for instance, was said to have muttered over and over during his last days, "The curse of the pharaohs."[30] The story was a complete fabrication, but this article and others like it fueled the fire of public opinion so that week by week, month by month, and year by year, the legend of King Tut's curse grew.

Did You Know?

According to one theory, as many as six of the mysterious deaths surrounding King Tut's tomb may have been the work of a serial killer who targeted people who were connected with the expedition.

More Deaths

It did not help matters that after the tragedies of the first year, additional people who had had contact with Tutankhamun's tomb met unfortunate and sometimes spectacular ends. All of these deaths were reported widely in the press. Each one was linked to the curse of King Tut in florid, hysterical prose.

The second wave of deaths began in early 1924, when a radiologist named Archibald Douglas-Reid became the next alleged victim of the curse. Douglas-Reid had been summoned to X-ray King Tut's mummy. He fell ill the day after performing this task and was dead three weeks later.

A British military general, Sir Lee Stack, was the next to succumb. Stack was commander in chief of the British-controlled Egyptian army during a period of political unrest. As a high-ranking official, he had been one of the first guests of honor to visit Tutankhamun's tomb. While driving to work he was shot several times on November 19, 1924, and he died of his wounds the next day.

More integral to the archaeological effort was Arthur Mace, an Egyptologist who worked closely with Carter after Tut's tomb was first opened. Mace helped by cataloging the items in the tomb and making sure they were removed safely. He became sick after about a year of this work and was forced to leave Egypt. He never recovered his good health; he died in 1928, after writing a letter claiming that he had been poisoned by arsenic.

Two more seemingly related deaths occurred in 1929. The first death was that of Richard Bethell, Lord Carnarvon's personal secretary and one of the first people to enter Tutankhamun's tomb. Bethell was found smothered in his bed at an exclusive London gentlemen's club. That same year also saw the death of yet another Carnarvon relative—Mervyn Herbert, Lord Carnarvon's youngest half brother. Herbert contracted malarial pneumonia on a trip through Europe and died shortly afterward. He had had nothing to do with Tutankhamun's discovery and had not even visited the tomb. But according to the press, his family connection to Carnarvon was enough to trigger the curse of King Tut.

Spectacular Stories

These stories, while curious, were not as spectacular as the two most gossip-worthy Tut-related incidents of the time. One such incident was the 1924 suicide of Hugh Evelyn-White, a British archaeologist who had assisted Carter with various tasks. According to later researchers, Evelyn-White was probably despondent over the death of a close friend, but newspapers ignored that

The removal of treasures such as this stunning pendant and necklace from Tutankhamun's tomb was believed by some to have brought down the ancient ruler's curse on those who disturbed his resting place.

fact and came up with their own version of events. They claimed that Evelyn-White was a superstitious man who had been nervous about a pharaoh's curse from the beginning. They said he became increasingly agitated in the year after the tomb's opening as misfortune befell various expedition members. He finally grew so fearful, the newspapers reported, that he took his own life. They further claimed he had written a note that left no doubt about the reach of the dire warnings from the tomb. The note supposedly read, "I have succumbed to a curse that forces me to disappear."[31]

The other incident was not fatal, but it was so curious that it generated endless chatter. In 1925 Carter sent a friend named Sir Bruce Ingham a macabre gift: a paperweight consisting of a mummified hand wearing a scarab bracelet. On the bracelet was inscribed the saying, "Cursed be he who moves my body. To him shall come fire, water, and pestilence."[32] Shortly after Ingham received this gift, his house burned to the ground. When he went to have it rebuilt, the foundations were washed away in a flash flood. Although this hand did not belong to Tutankhamun, it was all the same in the public mind. Ingham's misfortune, people thought, was clearly the result of Tutankhamun's ancient curse.

A Lingering Effect

In the ten years after the discovery and opening of Tutankhamun's tomb, these and other incidents had been so well publicized that people were ready to believe anything. The newspaper furor died down over the decades, but every now and then something happened to breathe new life into the curse of King Tut.

One story involves a man named Mohammed Mahdy. In 1977 Mahdy, then the head of the Egyptian Antiquities Organization, signed a contract permitting fifty objects from Tut's tomb to travel to the United States and England. On his way home from the office that very day, Mahdy was struck by a car and killed.

A Pop Culture Phenomenon

The discovery of King Tut's tomb coincided with the beginning of the mass media age. News outlets around the world were eager to share Carter's ongoing finds through written pieces, photographs, and filmed news clips. This publicity captured the public's attention, resulting in worldwide Tut mania. More popular in death than he probably ever was in life, the boy king inspired new fashions in music, clothing, fine art, film, furniture, and even architecture.

Women's fashion was particularly impacted by the so-called Nile style. Fabrics were printed with Egyptian-inspired patterns, such as hieroglyphs. Evening dresses in a mummy-wrap style were all the rage. Jewelry was modeled directly on relics from Tut's tomb, and hairstyles and makeup echoed the looks seen in ancient Egyptian images and statuary.

Hit songs also kept King Tut in the public eye—or ear, as the case may be. The novelty tune "Old King Tut," performed by Billy Jones and Ernie Hare, was a smash hit in 1923. But this song was far from the last to feature Tutankhamun. Perhaps the most popular was the 1978 hit "King Tut," performed by comedian Steve Martin and the Toot Uncommons backup band. Originally presented as a skit on the television show *Saturday Night Live*, the song eventually reached number seventeen on Billboard's Hot 100 chart and sold over 1 million copies as a single. This surprise success is a testament to the world's fascination with any and all things Tut.

Another account concerns Mahdy's successor, Gamal Mehrez. During an interview, Mehrez was asked what he thought about the idea of a pharaoh's curse. "I've been working as an archaeologist for the last thirty years, I've discovered temples, tombs, and mummies, and I'm still healthy,"[33] Mehrez said with a laugh. The next day, he dropped dead of a heart attack.

A Deep Belief

Although new stories surface every once in a while, archaeologists tend to dismiss them. They point out that if King Tut and his fellow pharaohs were truly out for revenge, there would be no Egyptologists left by now. They cite facts and figures to show that millions of people have been unharmed by a brush with

Egypt's ancient dead. Despite this data, belief in the curse of King Tut remains strong, fueled in large part by media coverage and speculation. Even the deepest believers concede that most people can and do dodge the pharaohs' wrath, but they see the curse as a kind of ancient Egyptian lottery. Millions may play without result, but someone has to win—or, in this case, lose.

Lord Carnarvon's descendants seem to hold this view. In a recent interview, the wife of Carnarvon's great-grandson discussed her feelings on the matter. "A member of the Carnarvon family never tempts fate. We don't know everything, those of us living here on earth. We can't see the whole picture. So I just tread carefully,"[34] she said. Like many others, Lady Carnarvon has read or heard many of the stories—and even in modern times, she is reluctant to dismiss King Tut's curse out of hand.

CHAPTER FIVE

Is the Curse Real?

All these years later, people still disagree on the reality of the curse of King Tut. Many people believe in this idea deeply and wholeheartedly. Others categorically reject the notion. Still others are unsure. They think there probably is no curse—but on the other hand, they note that there have been a lot of strange and seemingly unexplainable incidents involving ancient Egyptian tombs.

Many scientists and skeptics have tried to settle this question. They have challenged the idea of Tutankhamun's curse through logic, research, argument, statistics, and scientific studies. This data attempts to separate fact from fiction and shed some much-needed light on the potential existence of a pharaoh's curse.

Tomb Toxins

One prominent theory states that ancient Egyptian tombs did, in fact, kill people—but not through any supernatural means. Instead, the tombs contained long-dormant poisons of various sorts. These poisons may have been deadly, but they were not the work of angry spirits.

Known as the tomb toxin theory, this idea was first put forth during the mid-1980s by physician Caroline Stenger-Phillip. In a doctoral thesis, Stenger-Phillip suggested that the fresh fruits and vegetables placed in the pharaohs' tombs rotted, then became infested with a deadly type of mold. This mold spread throughout the tomb and released its dangerous spores for thousands of years. When archaeologists entered this toxic environment, they did not realize that they were sucking these spores into their lungs with each breath. This contamination led to a condition called allergic alveolitis, which is a severe and sometimes fatal inflammation of the tiny air sacs in the lungs. "[They] came to look for gold and treasures and paid no attention to the pink, gray and green patches of fungi on the walls. That's what killed some of them,"[35] Stenger-Phillip explained in a 1985 interview.

This theory seemed reasonable, and other scientists soon expanded upon it. They added other substances, including some that can cause fatal infections, to the list of potential tomb toxins. The list includes certain molds that are known to grow on mummies and dangerous bacteria such as pseudomonas and staphylococcus, which sometimes grow on tomb walls. They also pointed out that certain embalming chemicals, such as ammonia, formaldehyde, and hydrogen sulfide, can be harmful to human health. Yet another potentially harmful substance is hematite dust, a fine powder that the ancient Egyptians dumped liberally throughout the pharaohs' tombs to choke and discourage robbers. If inhaled, this powder might clog the lungs and lead to health problems.

At a glance, the tomb toxin idea sounds plausible. A deeper examination, however, shows that most of the facts do not fit the theory. The large majority of alleged curse victims did not die quickly of respiratory-related conditions. But a few did—and in these isolated cases, the tomb toxin theory may possibly hold some merit. "There is science behind the fact that when you are disturbing deposits that haven't been mucked around in a while, it's at least conceivable that you can expose yourself to some evil stuff,"[36] says Kenneth Feder, a professor of archaeology at Central Connecticut State University.

Many Survivors

If toxins account for some small percentage of the mysterious deaths surrounding King Tut's tomb, how are the non-illness-related events to be explained? The murders, suicides, assassinations, accidents, and general mayhem that occurred in the aftermath of Carter's expedition seem, to some people, to be more than purely coincidental. There were just too many untoward incidents to chalk up to chance.

A careful examination of the facts, however, suggests otherwise. It is particularly interesting to look at the people most likely to be affected by a pharaoh's curse—those who were directly involved in unearthing and opening Tutankhamun's tomb. According to a 1934 survey by Egyptologist Herbert Winlock, twenty-six people were present when the tomb was first opened, and of these, six died within the next ten years. A total of twenty-two people were present at the opening of Tut's sarcophagus, and two of these people died within the next ten years. A further ten people were present when Tut's mummy was unwrapped, and all of these people survived the following decade. This death rate, says Winlock, is completely reasonable over a ten-year span for the number of people involved.

As the man most responsible for the disruption of Tutankhamun's repose, Howard Carter was arguably the person most

Tutankhamun's sarcophagus is shown here in 2016 during further research on the tomb. Some experts have hypothesized that a deadly mold from rotted food may have been the cause of the illnesses and deaths of many of those involved in the tomb's plundering.

likely to be cursed. The archaeologist spent untold hours inside the tomb. During this time he ushered thousands of visitors in and out, and he stripped the tomb of its treasures. He also managed to accidentally decapitate Tut's mummy and detach its arms and legs while trying to remove the brilliant gold burial mask. All of these actions should have brought the wrath of Tutankhamun raining down upon Carter's head if, indeed, a curse existed. But Carter experienced nothing unfortunate during or after his tenure in Egypt. He survived for seventeen years after opening Tut's tomb, finally dying of natural causes in 1939 at the then ripe old age of sixty-four.

Those who believe in the curse of the pharaohs are quick to cite the many misfortunes that befell people with minor connections to King Tut. It is true that many deaths and accidents did occur in this group. But skeptics point out that thousands upon thousands of people trooped in and out of Tut's tomb soon after it was opened. Countless others handled artifacts from the tomb or were involved in some other minor way. In a group this large, tragedies are inevitable. Attributing each and every one of these incidents to King Tut is unreasonable and creates the perception of connections that are unlikely to exist.

Statistical Studies

Although it is impossible to prove or disprove connections like these, statistical analysis can shed some light on the probabilities involved. In 2002 a medical researcher named Mark R. Nelson did just such an analysis. Nelson combed through Carter's notes and extracted the names of all individuals from Western countries who were listed as being in Egypt when the tomb was opened. He further separated these individuals into two groups: those

Ever since Tutankhamun's tomb was opened in 1922, members of the public have been eager to see its contents with their own eyes. They have been able to satisfy this desire since 1961, when a traveling exhibition of Tut's treasures started working its way around the world. Called *Tutankhamun Treasures*, the show featured thirty-four artifacts. Between 1961 and 1966 the exhibition made multiple stops in America, Canada, France, and Japan, attracting many millions of visitors along the way.

Encouraged by the success of this tour, Egyptian officials have organized several successful follow-ups. *The Treasures of Tutankhamun* featured fifty objects and toured from 1972 until 1981. *Tutankhamun and the Golden Age of the Pharaohs* featured a different set of fifty objects, along with seventy other artifacts of the era, and toured from 2004 until 2011. *Tutankhamun: The Golden King and the Great Pharaohs* featured several objects from Tut's tomb, along with other items from the Valley of the Kings, and toured from 2008 until 2013. The final tour, *King Tut: Treasures of the Golden Pharaoh*, is currently under way and features 166 objects from Tut's tomb. The show is expected to run through 2025. When it ends, Egyptian officials say Tut's relics will return to the Egyptian Museum in Cairo, never to tour again.

who were directly involved with the tomb and those who were not. He then used statistical methods to compare life expectancy between the two groups.

This analysis revealed that there were, indeed, some differences. In particular, people who had entered Tut's tomb died on average about eight years sooner than those in the other group. But the Tut group was much older than the other group, and its members were almost exclusively male. When these differences were accounted for statistically, the gap virtually disappeared. Nelson found that there was an 87 percent chance that any differences in age at death were due to chance, and a 95 percent chance that length of survival was random. He concluded that "there was no significant association between exposure to the mummy's curse and survival and thus no evidence to support the existence of the mummy's curse."[37]

Carnarvon Revisited

When confronted with statements like this, believers often point to the death of Lord Carnarvon and the many strange events that accompanied it. It is simply too much to believe, they say, that all of these bizarre and tragic things happened by coincidence. Some supernatural force—namely, the wrathful spirit of King Tut—must have orchestrated Carnarvon's peculiar final days. His death, in particular, seemed highly suspicious.

A closer look at Carnarvon's life, however, makes his death seem much less mysterious. It turns out that Carnarvon had been in poor health since 1901, when he was severely injured in an automobile accident. Sickly, weak, and slow to heal, he had begun spending his winters in sunny Egypt to avoid the damp, chilly English weather. Through the subsequent years, as his interest in Egyptian archaeology blossomed, Carnarvon continued to spend a great deal of time in Egypt, but he never fully regained his health. Already frail, he was quick to succumb to a chance infection.

Did You Know?

Lord Carnarvon's English country home, Highclere Castle, was the main filming location for the popular television series *Downton Abbey.*

It should be noted, too, that penicillin was not discovered until 1928, five full years after Carnarvon's death. Without effective medicines, a bacterial infection was dangerous not only to those with weak constitutions but even to robustly healthy people who became infected. It seems incredible to the modern mind that an infected mosquito bite could kill a person. But in fact, this type of thing was not unusual during Carnarvon's time.

What about the rest of the story—Carnarvon's howling dog, the flickering lights of Cairo, and even Carter's dead canary? And why was Carnarvon's fatal mosquito bite in the identical position as a scar on Tutankhamun's cheek? There is a simple explanation for all of these odd stories: they were most likely made up by unscrupulous reporters to sell newspapers. As writer and self-appointed professional skeptic Brian Dunning points out, not one of these tales came directly from Carter or any of his expedition members. They "are found only in . . . unreliable newspaper reports and so can be considered anecdotal at best,"[38] he says in an article investigating claims of King Tut's curse. Today these stories have been repeated so many times that they have taken on the weight of fact, but when they were first published, they were probably more along the lines of ghost stories that the writers did not expect to be taken too seriously.

An Expert Opinion

For an expert opinion on the curse of the pharaohs, few people seem more qualified than Zahi Hawass. Perhaps the world's best-known Egyptologist, Hawass has served as the head of Egypt's Supreme Council of Antiquities (formerly the Egyptian Antiquities Organization) and also as the country's minister of antiquities. During the course of his fifty-year career, Hawass has participated in countless excavations and has handled every sort of ancient Egyptian artifact, including mummies. Many of his colleagues also

Egypt's former minister of antiquities, Zahi Hawass (center), examines Tutankhamun's mummy in 2005. Over his fifty-year career, Hawass says he has experienced many mysterious events connected with tomb excavations.

handle mummies and their so-called grave goods. If furious pharaohs are actually smiting the living from the afterworld, surely Hawass would have seen or experienced these curses firsthand.

Hawass confesses that he has seen some strange things in the course of his work. He relates one tale about carrying ancient relics to a museum in 1969, at the beginning of his career. Immediately after delivering the relics, he got a phone call telling him that one of his aunts had died. The next year he delivered more relics, and then discovered that one of his uncles had passed away. The third year, he was getting ready to make another delivery when he received a telegram notifying him that a cousin had been killed in an accident. "Reason, of course, told me that the deaths in my family were coincidences. Even so, that was the last year that I agreed to take the artifacts to the museum,"[39] he says in a memoir.

Did You Know?
True believers say that Howard Carter was, indeed, cursed by King Tut. His curse was to live a long life, watching as everyone he loved died one by one.

Hawass tells of another incident he found unnerving. He had discovered what appeared to be a family of mummies at one site. He sent the smaller mummies—presumably children—to a museum, but he left the others where he had found them. That night and for many nights following, Hawass was disturbed by nightmares that featured crying, linen-wrapped children. The dreams did not stop until Hawass reunited the smaller and larger mummies, after which point, he says, "the children never haunted me again."[40]

Hawass admits that incidents like these are strange, and he has occasionally wondered whether some sort of Egyptian magic might be at work. But Hawass's idea of magic is a very different matter than some sort of supernatural revenge. In all his years of excavating, Hawass says, "I have never had an experience that I would attribute to an ancient curse."[41] He is not willing to go quite so far as saying definitively that there is no curse. But even if a curse does somehow exist, he says, "I certainly do not fear it."[42]

Although it is unlikely that a real pharaoh's curse exists, the idea is alive and well on the big screen. Films about mummies started to emerge shortly after the discovery of Tutankhamun's tomb, and they have been a Hollywood fixture ever since.

The first major production was Universal Studios' 1932 film *The Mummy*, which starred the famously creepy actor Boris Karloff as a revived and seriously angry pharaoh named Imhotep. This film was such a success that it launched an entire franchise for Universal. The studio would go on to release thirteen more mummy-themed films, including the blockbuster *Mummy* series (1999, 2001, and 2008) starring Brendan Fraser. A 2017 film, also named *The Mummy*, had a big budget and big stars, including Tom Cruise, but it got poor reviews and disappointing results at the box office.

Besides Universal, many smaller studios have produced mummy movies. Some of them have featured exceptionally creative plots. Two Mexican films, *The Robot vs. the Aztec Mummy* (1959) and *Wrestling Women vs. the Aztec Mummy* (1964), are pretty much explained by their titles. Also from Mexico came *House of Terror* (1960), in which a resurrected mummy turned out to be a werewolf as well. In *Bubba Ho-Tep* (2002), an aging Elvis Presley teams up with president John F. Kennedy to fight an ancient Egyptian ghoul. And *The Kung-Fu Mummy* (2005) made an ambitious attempt to blend film genres, to the apparent delight of no one.

These films and others continue the time-honored tradition of sensationalizing mummies. The newspapers of Carter's day would be proud to see their work continued in such a spectacular way.

Living Forever

Most Egyptologists, if not all, hold a similar view. They are unconcerned about bringing down the wrath of the pharaohs any time they enter a new tomb, handle an artifact, or examine a mummy. This view is based partly on their personal experience—after all, they are still alive and unharmed—and partly on the evidence that has accumulated over the years. Between the studies of tomb toxins, the statistical analyses, and the debunking of the more fantastic stories, the logical conclusion is that the curse of King Tut simply does not exist.

The issue of pharaohs watching from the afterlife is a trickier question. Although it is impossible to prove or disprove such a notion, many people believe in life after death. They keep an open mind when it comes to such matters.

Yet even if Tutankhamun and his peers are watching, most Egyptologists say the idea of a curse makes no sense. "The greatest desire of the ancient Egyptians was that their names would live forever, granting them immortality," Hawass points out. "We as archaeologists dedicate our lives to bringing the names of the ancients back to life."[43] From Hawass's perspective, the pharaohs should be grateful, not angry.

If this is the case, then Lord Carnarvon and Howard Carter are surely smiled upon by King Tut. They snatched this minor, long-forgotten ruler from his three-thousand-year oblivion and turned him into a modern superstar. Curse or no curse, today everyone knows the name of Tutankhamun—and that is just the way the boy king would have wanted it.

SOURCE NOTES

Introduction: The Boy King

1. Quoted in Nicholas Reeves, *The Complete Tutankhamun*. London: Thames & Hudson, 1990, p. 10.

Chapter One: Egypt and the Pharaohs

2. Quoted in André Dollinger, "The Pharaoh—Man, Ruler and God," An Introduction to the History and Culture of Pharaonic Egypt, October 2004. www.reshafim.org.il.
3. Jackie S., "The Soul's Journey Through the Ancient Egyptian Afterlife," Owlcation, July 12, 2017. https://owlcation.com.
4. Quoted in Victoria Gill, "Ancient Egyptian Mummification 'Recipe' Revealed," BBC News, August 16, 2018. www.bbc.com.
5. Quoted in Joshua J. Mark, "Tomb Robbing in Ancient Egypt," Ancient History Encyclopedia, July 17, 2017. www.ancient.eu.
6. Quoted in Mark, "Tomb Robbing in Ancient Egypt."
7. Mark, "Tomb Robbing in Ancient Egypt."

Chapter Two: Exploring the Tombs of the Pharaohs

8. Quoted in Reeves, *The Complete Tutankhamun*, p. 38.
9. Quoted in Reeves, *The Complete Tutankhamun*, p. 48.
10. Quoted in T.G.H. James, *Howard Carter: The Path to Tutankhamun*. New York: Tauris Parke, 2006, p. 248.
11. Quoted in Matt Krantz, "Archaeologist Howard Carter: How Persistence Led Him to King Tut's Tomb," Investor's

Business Daily, July 6, 2018. www.investors.com.

12. Quoted in Michael R. King and Gregory M. Cooper, *Who Killed King Tut? Using Modern Forensics to Solve a 3,300-Year-Old Mystery*. Amherst, NY: Prometheus, 2006, pp. 77–78.
13. Quoted in King and Cooper, *Who Killed King Tut?*, p. 78.
14. Quoted in King and Cooper, *Who Killed King Tut?*, p. 79.
15. Quoted in King and Cooper, *Who Killed King Tut?*, p. 79.

Chapter Three: Strange Events

16. *New York Times*, "*Times* Man Views Splendors of Tomb of Tutankhamen," December 22, 1922. https://timesmachine.nytimes.com.
17. *New York Times*, "*Times* Man Views Splendors of Tomb of Tutankhamen."
18. Quoted in Unredacted, "Tutankhamun: The Curse of the Mummy," March 16, 2017. https://theunredacted.com.
19. Howard Carter, *Search, Discovery, and Clearance of the Antechamber,* vol. 1 of *The Tomb of Tutankhamun*. London: Bloomsbury, 2014, p. 92.
20. Quoted in Chris Wright, "Pharaoh and Loathing," *Discovery Channel Magazine India*, March 2015, p. 40.
21. Quoted in Mark Beynon, *London's Curse: Murder, Black Magic and Tutankhamun in the 1920s West End*. Stroud, UK: History, 2011. https://books.google.com.
22. Quoted in Unredacted, "Tutankhamun."
23. Howard Carter and Arthur Cruttenden Mace, *The Tomb of Tut-Ankh-Amen: Discovered by the Late Earl of Carnarvon and Howard Carter*. Vol. 2. Cambridge: Cambridge University Press, 2010, pp. xxv–xxvi.
24. Beynon, *London's Curse*.

Chapter Four: The Story Grows

25. Quoted in Linda Alchin, "Newspapers and the Curse of King Tut," History Embalmed, 2018. www.historyembalmed.org.
26. Quoted in University of Manchester, "90th Anniversary of the Curse of Tutankhamen: How a Modern Myth Was Born," April

4, 2013. www.manchester.ac.uk.

27. Quoted in Linda Alchin, "Sir Arthur Conan Doyle & the Curse of King Tut," History Embalmed, 2018. www.historyembalmed .org.

28. Quoted in *St. Louis Post-Dispatch*, "Ancient Curse Recalled by Lord Carnarvon's Illness," March 21, 1923, p. 2.

29. *St. Louis Post-Dispatch*, "Ancient Curse Recalled by Lord Carnarvon's Illness."

30. Quoted in Roger Luckhurst, "The Curse of Tutankhamen? Pure Invention," *Telegraph* (London), April 5, 2013. www .telegraph.co.uk.

31. Quoted in Aquiziam, "The Curse of Tutankhamun Facts," May 29, 2017. www.aquiziam.com.

32. Quoted in Aquiziam, "The Curse of Tutankhamun Facts."

33. Quoted in Zahi Hawass, *Curse of the Pharaohs: My Adventures with Mummies*. Washington, DC: National Geographic, 2004, p. 41.

34. Quoted in Rod McPhee, "Downton Abbey Was Almost Ruined by the Curse of Tutankhamun as Highclere Family Discovered the Tomb," *Mirror*, October 14, 2016. www.mirror.co.uk.

Chapter Five: Is the Curse Real?

35. Quoted in Milan Ruzicka, "Pharaoh's Curse—an Allergy to Mold?," AP News, July 30, 1985. www.apnews.com.

36. Quoted in Brian Handwerk, "Egypt's 'King Tut Curse' Caused by Tomb Toxins?," *National Geographic,* May 6, 2005. www .nationalgeographic.com.

37. Mark R. Nelson, "The Mummy's Curse: Historical Cohort Study," *British Medical Journal,* December 2002, vol. 325, no. 7378, pp. 1482–4.

38. Brian Dunning, "King Tut's Curse!," Skeptoid, June 24, 2008. https://skeptoid.com.

39. Hawass, *Curse of the Pharaohs*, p. 72.

40. Hawass, *Curse of the Pharaohs*, p. 80.

41. Hawass, *Curse of the Pharaohs*, p. 121.

42. Hawass, *Curse of the Pharaohs*, p. 9.

43. Hawass, *Curse of the Pharaohs*, p. 20.

FOR FURTHER RESEARCH

Books

Paul Harrison, *The Curse of the Pharaohs' Tombs: Tales of the Unexpected Since the Days of Tutankhamun*. Barnsley, UK: Pen & Sword, 2017.

Zahi Hawass and Sandro Vannini, *Tutankhamun: The Treasures of the Tomb*. New York: Thames & Hudson, 2018.

Kerrie Logan Hollihan, *Creepy and True: Mummies Exposed!* New York: Abrams Books for Young Readers, 2019.

Bridget McDermott, *Decoding Egyptian Hieroglyphs: How to Read the Secret Language of the Pharaohs*. London: Chartwell, 2016.

James L. Neibaur, *The Monster Movies of Universal Studios*. Lanham, MD: Rowman & Littlefield, 2017.

Lorna Oakes and Lucia Gahlin, *Ancient Egypt: An Illustrated History*. Leicester, UK: Lorenz, 2018.

Internet Sources

Chip Cooper, "A Most Merry and Illustrated History of Howard Carter and the Discovery of the Tomb of King Tutankhamun," CooperToons, November 9, 2018. www.coopertoons.com.

Bryan Hill, "Tomb Curses of Ancient Egypt: Magical Incantations of the Dead," Ancient Origins, June 13, 2015. www.ancient-origins.net.

James Hoare, "The Facts Behind the Curse of Tutankhamun: Fake News from Beyond the Grave," History Answers, May 3, 2017. www.historyanswers.co.uk.

Joshua J. Mark, "Tomb Robbing in Ancient Egypt," *Ancient History Encyclopedia*, July 17, 2017. www.ancient.eu.

Rod McPhee, "Downton Abbey Was Almost Ruined by the Curse of Tutankhamun as Highclere Family Discovered the Tomb," *Mirror*, October 14, 2016. www.mirror.co.uk.

Matthew Shaer, "The Controversial Afterlife of King Tut," *Smithsonian Magazine*, December 2014. www.smithsonianmag.com.

Websites

Ancient Origins (www.ancient-origins.net). This excellent site has a wealth of information on the major societies and events of humankind's past.

Aquiziam (www.aquiziam.com). This site explores the secrets of the human mind and the world. It includes an excellent section on Tutankhamun.

History Embalmed (www.historyembalmed.org). This site examines all aspects of Tutankhamun, from his biography to the discovery of his tomb and beyond.

Museum of Unnatural Mystery (www.unmuseum.org). Read about the curse of King Tut and other historical mysteries on this site.

Tour Egypt (www.touregypt.net). This site has links to over one hundred professional photographs of objects recovered from Tutankhamun's tomb.

INDEX